Published by Fusion Dynamics and You LLC
www.fdyconsultants.com

ISBN: 978-1-960973-08-5

Welcome!

DR. KINDALL BUNDY, MBA, QMHP, CDP

Dr. Kindall Bundy, pioneered the practice of business 20 + years, enhancing businesses and organizations within the surrounding counties of Richmond, Virginia. All before taking innovation to new heights, researching, inquiring, and implementing mindful resources. Later, compiled data and launched FD&Y Consultants, a corporation that has identified the need for guidance assisting youthful individuals, professionals, and corporations. Dr. Kindall Bundy's focus is directed toward skill-set development needed to enhance forward-thinking business planning, independent skill development, community enhancement, supportive resources, and succession planning.

FD&Y CONSULTANTS	2024

Contents

* Introduction

Who...Is Your Audience?

What... Are the Visuals you want to be displayed?

When...To Release Information Learned?

1 Beginners Toolkit for Blogging

2 Tell What You Know Through Blogging

3 The Art of Blogging

4 Write the Vision and Make a Plan

5 Think...Brainstorming

6 Knowledge Sharing is Expensive

7 Game Changing

Introduction

Are you a learner at heart with a passion for sharing your knowledge and experience with others? Then blogging might just be the perfect platform for you! With careful consideration of your words, you can use your blog to convey your thoughts, feelings, opinions, and everything in between.

Did you know that blogs have been around for over 20 years? The first blog was created by a student named Justin Hall in 1994. It was a simple platform for him to publish his writing, consisting of short posts that included a link and his thoughts on the content within. Since then, the nature of blogs has undergone incredible transformations, making them one of the most popular mediums for sharing information and ideas. Embrace the art of blogging and start your journey today!

In August 1998, Jonathan Dube became the first journalist to blog about Hurricane Bonnie in North Carolina, marking a significant turning point for the publishing industry. Blogging became an excellent platform for community members to express their opinions and comment on each other's writing. With no upfront financial costs, anyone could create an account with blog providers and publish their blogs for free.

Blogging has become crucial for individuals and organizations to share their expertise and increase global visibility. However, I would like to point out that not everyone who blogs will achieve worldwide fame. Attracting a broader audience may require extensive marketing efforts.

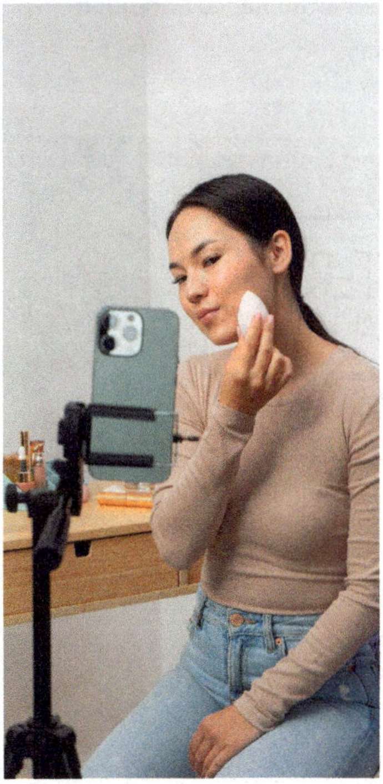

In 2002, blogging headed for a significant turn. People also started to make monetary profits from their blogs with sites like BlogAds, a precursor to Google AdSense. Business blogs came about shortly after and were created to advertise the services or products of various types of businesses to increase in-person and online sales.

In 2005, Garrett Graff became the first blogger in the history of blogging to be granted a press pass for the White House. This, along with the release of the Huffington Post in the same year, put blogging onto the political map and provided a new level of legitimacy as a media source. With blogs, entrepreneurs can establish a name in the virtual market through articles that can be useful in the reader's life.

From there, blogging made Medium waves by introducing new ways to pay content creators in the blogging industry. They introduced a subscription model and, in 2017, replaced several of their competitors in the industry, rising on the charts to be one of the leading options in their field with a partner program. Since 2023, Medium has been home to thousands of blogs with various levels of success, and they even employ some writers directly.

WHO...IS YOUR AUDIENCE?

Understanding your audience is crucial for a successful blog. You need to take into account the age of your readers, followers, and fans, as they are the ones who will help elevate your blog. While bloggers often cover a variety of topics, their main goal is to be acknowledged, read, and recognized for their efforts. Therefore, it is essential to maintain consistency, clarity, and knowledge in your blog. The ultimate aim is to ensure clarity and maintain understanding for your readers.

WHAT... ARE THE VISUALS YOU WANT TO DISPLAY?

Visual elements are crucial for engaging visual learners and enhancing comprehension. Creating visually appealing content is vital to cater to readers. Emphasizing key points visually can enhance understanding.

KNOWLEDGE SHARING

When creating content, it's important to be mindful of your audience. Avoid using profanity, as it may limit your reach to adult viewers. Instead, focus on sharing well-researched and valuable information to engage a larger audience and build brand longevity.

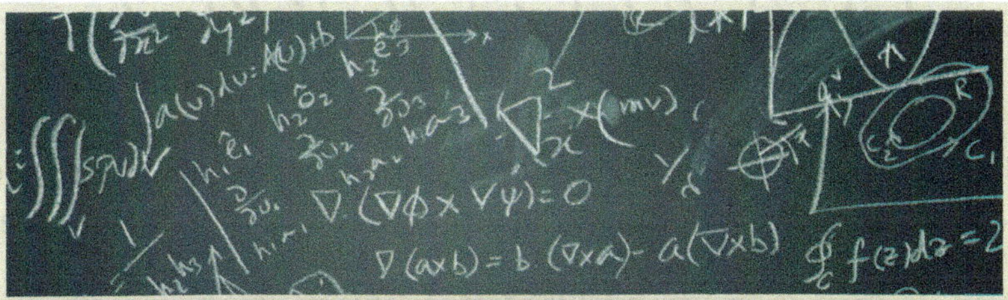

DO NOT BE OVERLY INFORMATIVE

In today's fast-paced society, people have very limited leisure time. However, recent data suggests a growing interest in reading, with more people planning to read books in 2023 compared to 2022. According to recent statistics, 64% of readers have set a goal to read more books in the upcoming year than in the previous year. Therefore, individuals need to be selective in choosing what they read to make the most of their time.

When creating blog content, ensure it covers the essential elements: who, what, when, where, and how. Utilize www.grammarly.com for all-encompassing writing support, covering grammar, spelling, style, and tone, to effectively convey your message.

ASK QUESTIONS OF YOUR AUDIENCE

In light of the Covid-19 pandemic, social isolation has significantly increased. As a result, people have sought informal connections and spontaneous interactions more than ever before. Creating an interactive space for content, such as blogging, is crucial for allowing dialogue to develop. It offers a unique audience and engagement experience, which sets it apart from mainstream social platforms.

What's Next?

This is just a page for you to fill the computer with ideas, thoughts, questions, concerns or research topics that you plan to explore at a later date.

Blog Vision Planner

Write the Mission
& Start Plan B

Services &
Products
*Consider Costs

First Year
Blog Goal
*Consider Costs

Blog Vision Planner

Write the Mission
& Start Plan A

Services &
Products
*Consider Costs

First Year
Blog Goal
*Consider Costs

1

Beginners Toolkit for Blogging

Creating Innovative Income Streams with Blogging
Many groundbreaking ideas arise from difficult circumstances. Moving from aspiring to become the top journalist at a prestigious magazine to managing a platform where your voice can resonate with a larger audience has ignited a fresh surge of energy, creativity, and open dialogue of ideas. Coming together in a common space to express thoughts you wish to share and potentially inspire others has encouraged innovation.

Different styles, formats, and settings are available for blogs to meet the diverse preferences of users. Several blogging platforms come with pre-built features like hyperlinks, plain text, and images. Moreover, some specific platforms allow users to integrate videos and desired content from other platforms into their blogs.

Audio blogging is a popular alternative to written blogs, allowing bloggers to make their content more accessible through spoken word entries. By using audio content instead of written content, bloggers can create a unique, engaging experience for their audience.

A blog typically includes several key components, such as the title, body, trackback, permanent link, and comments. The title is used to label your post, while the body contains the main content. Trackback lets other websites link back to your blog, while permanent link gives each article you write a unique URL. Comments enable readers to leave feedback on your blog, encouraging engagement and discussion.

One of the best things about blogging is its simplicity. Unlike other websites with countless pages, blogs usually have just a few templates, making it easier for bloggers to create new content. With fixed settings for the title, post, category, and more, bloggers can quickly create new pages and publish their thoughts and ideas, with minimal fuss.

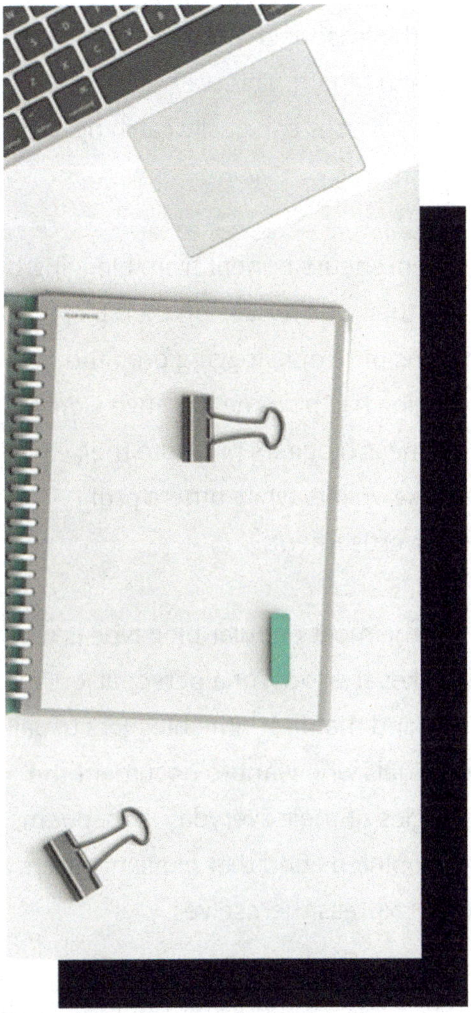

Blogging can allow individuals to express their insights and viewpoints on various subjects and interests.

- Some bloggers utilize their blogs for promotional purposes, such as showcasing their books.
- Others use their blogs to bring attention to current events, news, and crises.

Especially beneficial for first-time users, as it allows them to start blogging promptly. They have the option to select from various templates provided by blogging platforms.

Individuals looking to launch a blog can do so by joining a preferred blogging platform. Upon becoming members, they are automatically integrated into the blogging community.

Users can explore other bloggers' pages and link them back to their own blogs. Additionally, they can engage by commenting on posts from other members.

Blogging extends beyond personal use. Many blogs focus on specific themes such as sports, politics, philosophy, and social commentary and delve deep into their respective subjects.

Blogs today also play an essential part in education. Professors use blogging to document the lessons that they have discussed and taught. This way, students who have missed classes can easily catch up with their assignments.

Many entrepreneurs benefit from blogging by promoting their businesses on their blogs. With millions of people logging onto the net daily, blogging has become lucrative. Some online business bloggers promote their merchandise online, while others profit through advertisement.

But by far, the most popular blog type is the one that takes the form of a personal journal. This is the kind that first-time bloggers usually use. Individuals who want to document the daily struggles of their everyday lives, poems, rants, and opinions find that blogging offers a medium to express themselves.

Bloggers usually communicate within themselves. This is one of the appeals of blogging. It creates a community of people sharing their ideas, thoughts, and comments.

Blog directories contain blogs on topics, themes, and setups. First-time users who want to learn about the blogging world can browse several blogs using these directories to understand these blogging communities.

Blogging is a platform used worldwide. The blog is short for weblog. There are no rules when it comes to blogging. Bloggers have the freedom to express themselves however they want, and the best thing about blogging is that most blogging sites are free.

There are numerous blogging websites on the net. This gives first-time users the option of joining a blogging community that appeals to their interests.

Just search any blogging directory, and you'll find many blogging sites available on the net. It's easy to find a blogging directory because it is organized according to category.

This way, you would get precisely what you are after. Blogging is really for everyone. It is fun, simple and easy.

The Setup Process

Blogging is a lucrative source of profit, and blogs are easy to set up and maintain. Imagine a life where you are paid to write on stuff that interests you, whenever you want, wherever you are.

Blogging's flexibility makes it easy to kick back, relax, and go on vacation whenever you like.

In this article, we will look into the profitability of a blog and set up a blog of our own at no cost! Interested? Read on!

First, we need to obtain a blog. There are several options: host a blog on your domain or get a free blog. For starters, let's talk about free blogs.

You can obtain a free blog at blogger.com or the newer (and better!) wordpress.com. If you are a techie, you must have heard of WordPress, a robust and infinitely expandable free blog engine.

Google owns Blogger.com, so it will be detected on Google's radar faster, and you will be indexed faster. Wordpress.com, however, is a relatively new option, so I have no comparison on the speed of getting indexed by search engines.

However, WordPress is better because it has more advanced features, such as Trackbacks and Categories. You can also manage your sidebar links more efficiently (more about this later).

Get a free blog at either Blogger.com or WordPress.com. Then, familiarize yourself by posting your first post on your blog and tinkering around with the options and templates.

Here are a few common "blog-related" words to help you out:

Permalink – Permalink stands for permanent link, a URL (uniform resource locator) that leads to an individual post you make in your blog.

Trackback – When you post about someone else's blog post elsewhere, your post will show up in their "trackback" section. This feature, however, is not available with a Blogger.com account.

Pinging—Blogging and pinging seem to be paired almost every time either one is mentioned nowadays. Pinging is notifying a particular aggregator whenever your blog is updated so that the aggregator may show the newest pos**t** on their website. This is a valuable way to gain traffic, which we shall discuss later.

In the following chapters, we will discuss how people can profit from a blog and offer tips on writing posts that keep visitors glued and coming back for more!

Brain Dump

This is just a page for you to brain-dump any ideas, thoughts, questions, concerns or "research topics" that you plan to explore later.

Think Tank

2

Tell What You Know About Blogging

A business blog is an incredible online marketing tool that saves you thousands of dollars but provides great business opportunities in just one click.

Blogs are user-friendly, customizable and flexible medium for disseminating useful information for effectively positioning your products in the market.

Companies engaging in business blogging have a definite edge over their competitors.

WORD-OF-MOUTH

In a survey, there are currently 14 million blogs with 80,000 more being added each day and about 30 percent of the 50 million users are

Blog readers. Imagine how much gain your company will have if your products are advertised through blogs.

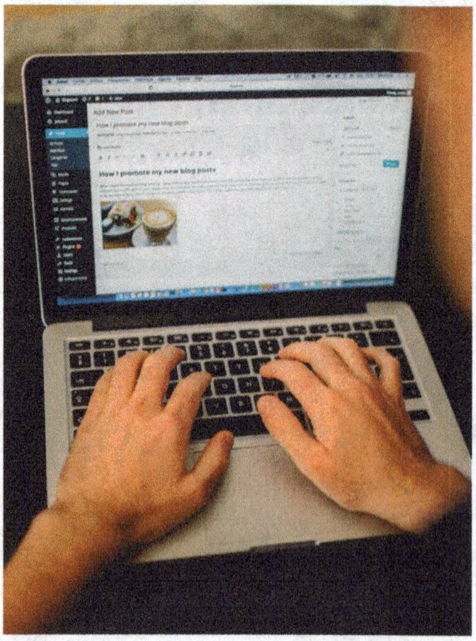

With Internet, information spreads so quickly especially if an impressive write-up goes with your product. Soon your blogs will be passed on to hundreds of possible customers.

AWARENESS AND LOYALTY

Open communication with your customers creates trust and loyalty among them. Being there to respond to their questions and comments make them all the more willing to try your products and services.

FEEDBACK

Blogs are good for product research and reviews. It would be easier to improve your products if you observe your customers' thinking and behavioral patterns. You can also take immediate action to address your customers' concerns.

COMMUNITY HALO-EFFECT

Bloggers are reasonable, friendly and helpful. They are more than willing to create blogosphere of comments regarding your product. The only thing you have to do is embrace and take active part in the culture and your product will surely be considered in their next stop to the supermarket.

For better marketing results, actively promote your business blogs by submitting your blogs to blog search sites and directories. Do not forget to paste in with your blogs, your URL.

Be sure that your blogs contain exclusive information with value and are always updated to keep readers popping in, read up your blog, move on to the next and click on again for updates.

Blog is like a setup booth in the biggest trade show on earth every day. Marketing possibilities are just around the corner waiting to strike your sale scales up.

The Really Simple Syndication (RSS) feeds are important too in conjunction with your blogs to get the best benefits. Use effective keyword phrases to generate high ranking status in the search engine traffic. In this way you have better chances of people finding your website leading to your blogs. More traffic means more potential sales.

For this to be successful, you can use RSS for news update feeds which can be read through RSS reader application. This is a very useful tool for business and internet marketers as well.

If you are already convinced with the potentials of business blogs for marketing and targeting sales increase, your company is now ready to start blogging.

But first, you have to be in tune with your company's business objectives and determine if blogging will really help you achieve your goal.

Several blogs teach people the do's and don'ts of blogging; review and apply them! Include consumer-based blogs in your reading materials to give you an idea. Set up several test blogs right away. If your initial tryout with blogs worked well, you can start setting up your blogs.

If you are planning to start a blog, there are several important things that you should consider beforehand. First, you need to decide whether you want to use pre-designed templates that are provided by blog hosting services or if you want to hire an artist to create a unique layout that aligns with your company's identity and needs. Additionally, it's essential to choose topics that align with your business objectives, even if the results may sometimes contradict your set goals.

Also, it's crucial to take into account any legal issues that may arise while blogging, so it's highly recommended to include disclaimers and limitations of liabilities in your blog. Finally, it's a great idea to encourage your employees to use the blog site as well.

Corporate communication and the legal department are responsible for educating the senior management on how blogs might affect business, Creating blogging policies, setting limits on who gets to blog and what information is allowed to be made public, Avoiding outright marketing blogs, or you will shy away from your readers; Make content updated, relevant, and fresh; and, Reinforce the company's core values.

- Start blogging and complete 20 posts before going to marketing. Begin marketing.
- Regularly monitor the coming ins and outs of readers and get updates. Then, measure your results.

- Adjust if needed. You can always play with your designs in the blog site as long as it remains to match the company's identity.
- You should strive to be consistent with your topic all the time.
- Try to have unrelated topics with general and broad appeal.
- Schedule updates regularly. Monday, Wednesday, and Thursday would be best to update blogs.
- Once you have done all these things, you can ultimately enjoy the benefits of business blogging.

Blogging Is ...
The New Internet Marketing To

Blogging is a concept that started in late 90s. It used to be a way to comment an existing webpage, an opportunity for visitors and readers to react or voice out one's opinion on the said page.

What started as a single-sentence commentary has evolved into pages of personal take on just about anything and everything under the sun. As it continues to move forward, online advertising has tapped into the blog's potential.

Here are 5 reasons why you should use blogging as an Internet marketing tool:

BLOGGING IS SIMPLE

The simplest way to get your piece on the net is through blogging. No skills are necessary... an average adult can read and type, or at least click a mouse.

It's like having a virtual piece of paper and you just write your ideas, experiences, new products, and hope that the truth behind your articles comes out and entice your reader to also try your product.

If you have a PC and an Internet connection (who doesn't?) then you can blog and advertise.

BLOGGING IS AUTHENTIC

In this day and age, when advertising saturates our lives, we question the credibility of promoters' claims. However, in blogs, real people share their real-life experiences unscathed by paid advertising.

Reading blogs about first-hand product use is like talking to people about their first-hand experience. You want to buy a tried and tested product.

BLOGGING IS FREE

As of yet, blogging has not been established as a mainstream online advertising medium. Therefore, most websites view it as a supplement to their current marketing tools and make it available for free. This free web time can be a valuable bonus, especially for new businesses. However, it's worth noting that paid blog pages have the potential to generate more income for a growing business.

BLOGGING BUILDS CREDIBILITY

As you write more about your experiences with a particular product or industry, your readers will come to trust your posts as a reliable source of information. This will establish you as an expert in your field, leading to an increase in the number of visitors to your site and the number of bloggers who link to your content.

As your blog's readership base continues to expand, companies and professional organizations will inevitably notice. They will be eager to seize advertising opportunities on your page or to become an affiliate, offering you payment for every referral generated from your blog. So, be prepared for such offers and capitalize on them to maximize your blog's potential.

BLOGGING BUILDS YOUR MARKET

Blogging is a powerful tool that can help you reach a wider audience, even if you're not a Hollywood star. With the right strategies in place, you can turn your blog into a thriving platform that attracts readers from all over. Don't limit yourself to just your mom as your audience. Take the necessary steps to build your market and increase your readership. Start blogging today!wever, you can expand your readership by implementing strategies to build your market through blogging.

USING YOUR EMAIL

Blogging is becoming more popular than email for reaching and expanding a market. In today's fast-paced world, logging in and downloading emails can take longer than clicking on a blog site. You can encourage people to explore your site by using a short email message as a teaser for your blog. If your email is on a different subject, you can use your email signature to provide a link to your site.

USING SUBSCRIPTION

One simple method to obtain the email addresses of your readers is to offer them a chance to subscribe to your blog. To encourage readers to subscribe and share their email address, reserve some exclusive content for subscribers. However, it is important to use their email address responsibly, as you don't want to be perceived as a spammer by receiving comments on your blog.

UNDERSTANDING YOUR READERS

Conduct a simple survey for your readers to understand their profile and advertising preferences. Ask consumers to give you feedback on a post, an ad link, or a trial that you shared. In this way, it is like interviewing your readers without the commitment and intrusion of a face-to-face interview.

JOINING A BLOG NETWORK

A network of blogs is a group of interconnected blogs that share common interests, readership, payment methods, and more. It offers convenience and credibility by providing access to multiple authentic bloggers discussing a specific topic, which adds value compared to just one.

USING RSS

RSS, or Really Simple Syndication, is a rapidly expanding technology on the Internet. By including RSS feeds to your website, you can attract more readers and generate awareness of your content. Additionally, having a diverse range of feeds can make your blog more interesting and engaging.

If you want to give your business a boost, you can effectively use blogging as an Internet marketing tool.

Brain Dump

This is just a page for you to brain-dump any ideas, thoughts, questions, concerns or "research topics" that you plan to explore later.

Think Tank

3

The Art Of Blogging

Blogs have increased popularity over the years.

Blogging has become a popular way for individuals to express their thoughts and feelings, and for companies to share product news and reviews with consumers. It has also become a tool for internet marketing, as many people spend time reading blogs on topics they're interested in, including product reviews.

Previously, companies would place banners and links on popular websites or include them in newsletters and marketing letters, but now blogging has become a more effective way to reach out to potential customers.

However, the increasing popularity of blogging has raised concerns that people may rely too heavily on blogs for the latest news, which may not always be reliable or accurate.

While some people may consider relying on news reports from blogs to be untrustworthy, many tend to look for product reviews on blogs. Surprisingly, this method of obtaining information can be more reliable in some cases. While it is true that some journalists may get paid to write positive reviews about a particular product, bloggers typically write about their personal experiences with products and services from companies.

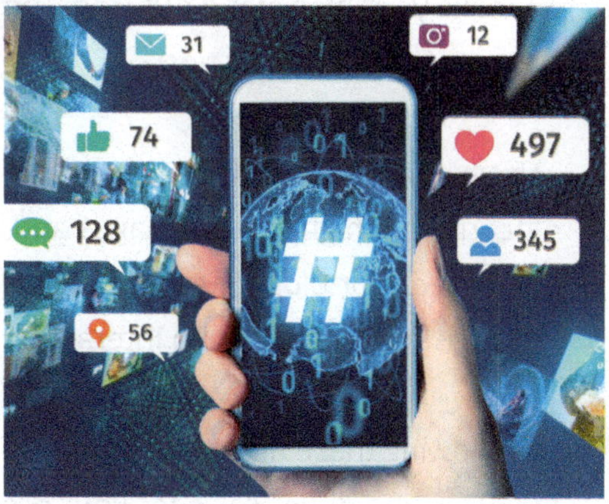

Blogging is a powerful marketing tool, and more people are starting their own blogs to leverage its potential. The key to success is to boost your blog traffic, which in turn will increase your product sales.

To increase your blog traffic, join affiliate programs or websites that list your blog under a specific search category or name. While advertising your blog on popular websites is also an option, it can be expensive and not recommended if you're just starting out.

If you're new to blogging, it's crucial to increase traffic to your site to maximize ads on your site. By choosing advertisers who pay for clicks or page views, you can earn while increasing your site's visibility.

To keep visitors engaged and coming back, you must create informative and engaging content and an eye-catching blog layout and design. You can create high-quality content yourself, or you can get the services of a professional web content writer to provide you with the necessary articles.

The layout and design of your blog play a significant role in attracting and retaining visitors. While most companies offering free blog hosting provide pre-selected templates, some allow customization that, if utilized correctly, can increase your blog traffic.

To make your blog stand out from the millions of blogs with standard designs, here are a few tips:

- Use a unique design that reflects your brand and messaging
- Incorporate high-quality images and videos to break up the text
- Optimize your blog for search engines by including relevant keywords
- Engage your readers with interactive features like polls or quizzes.

By following these tips, you can create a successful blog that attracts a loyal following and drives sales for your products.

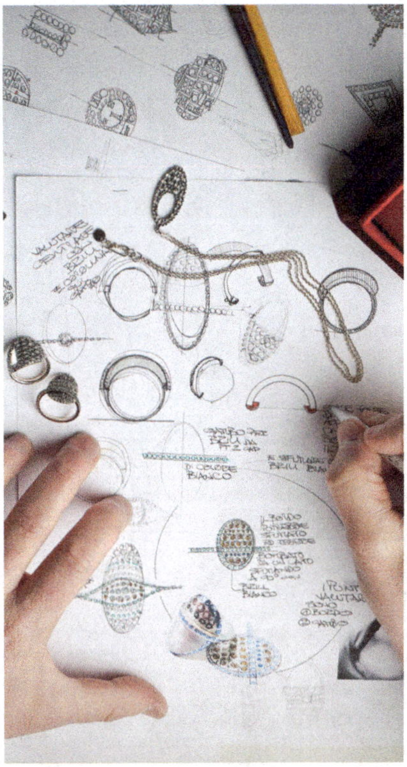

CUSTOMIZE THE BANNER

When you begin creating a blog using a blogging service or company, the banner design might seem generic and commonly used in many blogs. However, you can personalize your banner by designing a graphic that meets the required dimensions and adding your blog's title.

If you are unsure of your graphic design skills, you can buy professional-looking graphics online for less than $10. This will make your banner more attractive and give your blog a more refined appearance.

PERSONALIZING PHOTOS

When you create a blog post, it's recommended that you use your own photos to make it more personal. However, if you don't edit your photos before posting, you might miss out on the benefits that graphics can bring to your blog. By adding borders to your photos, you can give them a more professional look and improve the overall design of your blog. You can either choose a pre-made border or create your own to match your blog's style.

ADD A FAVICON

To give your website a more professional look, it's crucial to add icons to the address bar before the URL. Fortunately, it's a simple process that you can achieve with photo or graphic editing software.

INCLUDE RSS FEEDS

This is a cool way to inform people with newsreaders about your blog headlines. Tutorials on RSS feeds are available on the internet.

AUDIO MAKES YOUR BLOG MORE PERSONAL

Not only does audio personalizes the blog; it can also keep your visitors coming back. You can try having streaming radio stations, mp3 file or playlists loading with your blog.

ADVERTISEMENTS

If you have signed-up with Google Adsense, which I am sure you would like to do, make sure that the ads are conveniently placed that these will not hinder your readers' ease in accessing the information on your blog. Try using these tips and you can definitely increase and retain traffic on your blog.

Blog Hosts

Apart from chat rooms, instant messengers, and electronic mails created for communication and dialogue beyond turf are the emerging innovations that help humans build opportunities for interaction.

The need for a personalized, human-faced approach to building online communities is slowly changing the technological landscape of the Internet.

Blogs or blogging are the gift of Internet technology to people worldwide. These are updated posts, crop-up entries, or personalized life snippets of mundane or bizarre nature. For most, a "blog" is a personal, unedited, and authentic journal meant to be shared in an online community.

A blog site is where bloggers can publish anything: their thoughts, feelings, photos, special events, experiences, comments on issues, etc. It is more of an online diary with videos, links, documents, newsletters, and opinions on any topics you are interested in.

Blogs are made to welcome the insights and opinions of all and therefore, should not be written to sound intimidating and too formal.

This kind of blog is a sure way to put off the readers. In the basics of blogging, conversational tone would be more appropriate to reach the desired audience. Blogging is all about individuals reaching out to other individuals.

Having a blog has its own set of advantages:

FREEDOM OF EXPRESSION

If you want people to hear you out and give their own opinion, this is the best way to create a line of communication;

NETWORKING IS AT ITS BEST

Having a blog is a good platform for exchanging genuine ideas from consumers to you as the marketer of a specific product. Sound opinions and points of view are better than just showing the price quote;

EXCELLENT ADVERTISING PLATFORM

Blogging is a new way to advertise products, a refreshing change from the traditional advertising outlets and it is cost-effective.

GAUGING PUBLIC OPINION ON PRODUCTS AND SERVICES

The key is to use catchy titles and present new ideas in your content. This will ensure quick and repeated responses from your readers.

Blogs are excellent spots for the exchange of ideas between sellers and consumers. They are also good for measuring public opinion regarding services and products, as well as political and business matters.

USEFUL TOOL FOR INTERNAL COMMUNICATION

This will help your company to build a knowledge-based community of employees. Also good for harnessing employee relations and identifying human resource issues in advance.

Other benefits like search engine optimization (SEO) will help your blogs to be seen often by as many people as you wish. This is very good exposure for your products and services.

Many blog hosting services are available on the Internet. But the basic question is which one of the services will be the best to start off your business blog program?

It is imperative for businesspeople to stay up-to-date with the latest technological advancements that can help them leverage their marketing potential to the fullest. For novices, it is highly recommended to thoroughly analyze the services provided by different blog hosts. An ineffective business blogging strategy can severely damage marketing opportunities instead of boosting them.

A company should either host its blog service, pay a third-party to host the service, or set up a "blog aggregator page" and ask employees to select their blog hosting services individually. Individuals can choose from both free and paid services available in the market.

In order to achieve maximum marketing, public relations, and SEO potential, business blogs must have the latest blogging features. It is essential to remember that blogs must have the following fundamental elements:

Comments:

So that you know- welcoming comments provide an opportunity for dialogue. In business blogs, they are a suitable customer feedback mechanism. This helps develop better customer relations based on loyalty and trust. Blogging is an innovative way to converse with your customers.

Trackback:

This helps maximize company and product exposure. This service lets consumers contact you for more posts and updates without difficulty locating you.

If your blog is popular in a specific online community, chances are links to your blog site are everywhere, on other blog sites or websites.

RSS Feed:

Simple Syndication is sending the feed from your blog to the Internet and collecting it through various newsreaders and aggregators.

If your company is to establish a business blogging program, the hosting companies shortlisted for the services should offer considerable options.

Free blog hosting services are popular, but they are best suited for individual online journals. Paid blog hosting services offer unlimited packages that are best for your company's needs.

You may want to suggest checking out some blogs that use the host first, reading and examining their layout and design. Another important thing to consider is the host's reliable technical support.

After choosing the blog host, a team should be ready to plan the design and structure of the blog, as the team should:

Create a style that meets the needs of the audience.

Could you set up an open, credible tone?

Schedule weekly updates to the blog - ideally, a few times a week.

Include weblinks of other websites and blogs.

Blog posts should be in the "first person.

Focus on the business blog objective.

I want you to please maintain an honest, engaging conversational quality.

Remember, whatever the look, style, and content found on your blog reflects you and your company.

Brain Dump

This is just a page for you to brain-dump any ideas, thoughts, questions, concerns or "research topics" that you plan to explore later.

Think Tank

4

Write the Vision Make it Plain

Identifying barriers to blogging. Some barriers are visual, and others are not. This chapter introduces awareness.

Many people dream of blogging for profit, and this goal is within the reach of someone with average intelligence, a willingness to work hard, and a basic grasp of blogging technology. However, very few people reap the profits they want from their blogs.

Most people who attempt to make money with their blogs do not succeed for two reasons. Often, bloggers have unrealistic expectations of how fast their readership will grow and how much money they will make. When these expectations are unmet, the disappointment can crush the desire to continue blogging.

The other trap that many bloggers fall into is the need for more planning. If you want to turn a profit as a blogger, the key to success is to make a realistic plan and stick with it.

To succeed at blogging for profit, you will need a large readership. The higher your traffic, the more advertisers will agree to pay you.

However, cultivating the regular visitors you will need to make a profit isn't easy. As more and more blogs appear each day, having a great idea or a wonderful writing style is no longer enough to get attention. You need to be able to market your blog effectively.

Too many bloggers spend all of their time writing posts and almost no time marketing their projects. To be certain, updating as often as you can is a great way to keep your blog high on blogrolls and high in blog search engines like Technorati. Once your readers know that you update frequently, they will return to your site on a regular basis.

However, it does not matter how often you update if nobody is reading your page, so don't skimp on the time you spend drawing visitors to your site.

To make your dreams of blogging for profit a reality, try decreasing your number of posts and using time to draw new visitors by setting up link exchanges with other bloggers, making contacts in the blog community, and following other established modes of winning traffic.

Of course, even if you are a marketing genius or have an excellent idea for a blog, success will take a while. Building the kind of readership that blogging for profit requires takes time, and in all likelihood, it will be at least several months before you can turn much of a profit. Try to stay committed to your blogging project during this initial rough period.

To stay motivated, set goals for how often you will update and how many readers you want to attract, and then reward yourself for sticking with your plan.

LEARNING HOW TO MAKE MONEY BLOGGING

There are two major types of business models that entrepreneurs use to make money blogging. The first and most common way to turn a blog into a profit making machine is to sell advertising to different companies and brands who want to reach that blog's readers.

The second kind of money making blog is one that helps a single brand improve its image by creating positive associations between the blog and the product in the mind of consumers. Both kinds of blogs can make a lot of money, especially if the creator has a keen mind for marketing.

If you are blogging with the goal of selling advertising, there are two basic ways that you can go about recruiting sponsors who want to put ads on your site; you can let someone else do all of the legwork, or you can do the work yourself and keep all of the revenue.

Within the first group, many people make money blogging by selling space through Google's AdSense program. The advantages of this program are numerous, as it requires very little effort on the part of the blogger or webmaster to begin raking in profits.

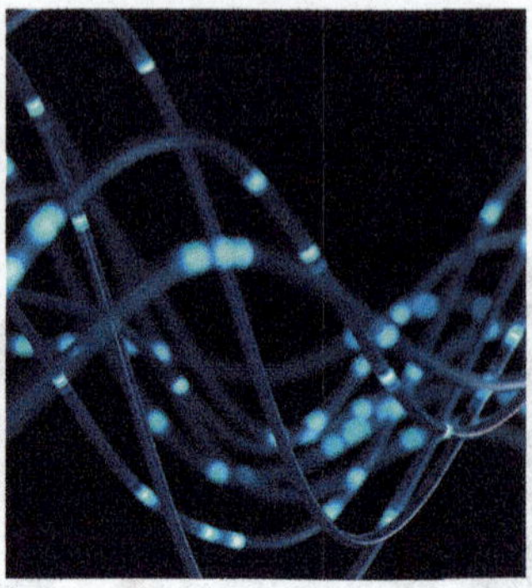

Within the first group, many people make money blogging by selling space through Google's AdSense program. This program has numerous advantages, as it requires very little effort on the part of the blogger or webmaster to begin raking in profits.

However, most people discover they make less money through this method than they hoped their blog would earn.

Selling advertising directly to companies that want to put banner ads or sponsored links on your blog can take quite a bit of time, but it is often fairly lucrative. If you have many contacts in industries related to your blog's topic, you may want to try this route.

People who have a strong sales background and are experienced at pitching proposals can make quite a bit of money by renting blog space to interested companies.

The most severe problem with this model is that you often have to build quite a sizable readership before you can attract advertisers, which can mean that you have to do several months of work before you start to make money blogging.

As blogging becomes a more lucrative business, many established companies are considering how they can participate.

Companies are capitalizing on the blog movement by having blogs that provide a kind of friendly face for their corporation. Often, a company will employ an established blogger to create a weblog designed specifically to appeal to that company's customers and to create positive associations with the brand in consumers' minds.

More than one writer who never even dreamed that they could make money blogging has been approached by a company and offered quite a pretty penny for this kind of gig.

Blogging Now = Money Now

If you already spend a fair amount of time blogging, money may come to you as soon as you ask. Once you have an established blog with a regular readership, it is easy to profit through advertising.

You can see income from your hobby almost overnight by hosting sponsored links or banners. Even if you did not start your blog intending to turn a profit, making supplementary income from your blog may be easier than you think.

Suppose your blog is on a subject that appeals to a demographic that advertisers strongly desire to reach. In that case, you will be more likely to be able to turn a significant profit on your blog than if your blog is on a relatively obscure subject that does not draw the kind of audience that advertisers need to appeal to. Of course, the only way to find out where you fall on this spectrum is to try hosting some ads. If you are already blogging, you have nothing to lose.

Brain Dump

This is just a page for you to brain-dump any ideas, thoughts, questions, concerns or "research topics" that you plan to explore later.

Think Tank

5

Think Brainstorming

Consistency is the key... updating your information is essential for your followers.

You will find fresh topics to write about, and this chapter will explain how to accomplish that goal.

We have discussed how to write attractively, so now we are going to discuss what we are going to write about. The very first option that I think a blogger should write on is a topic that he or she feels passionate about and is interested in.

You've chosen to make blogging your career because you want to escape a mundane job. Forcing yourself to write about something you're not interested in is as torturous as your mundane job!

The other reason I ask you to write about something you're passionate about is because your feelings and emotions show through your writing! If you feel indifferent to a particular subject but still write about it just for the sake of it, your readers will notice it. Remember the advice about writing with a personality? Forcing yourself to write will not establish a welcoming style at all.

Once you have chosen your central theme, start posting about it on your blog. Make it a habit to post at least once every day, even if it's only a comment on the newspaper article you read today. Think of yourself as a gigantic train.

It takes much effort to get you moving. First, you might budge an inch and trudge slowly until you finally reach your full speed. Then, it'll take much effort to stop you instead!

However, no matter how well you know your topic, your brain is bound to get exhausted over time, so here are methods for brainstorming content for your blog.

The best way to brainstorm is to see what other bloggers say about stuff happening in your field of discussion. And the very best way to find related blogs is to use blogsearch.google.com or technorati.com

There are other decent search tools, too; you must look around. You can also gather more knowledge on your subject from other blogs and comment on what others have to say on your own blog!

Once you've established contacts with other bloggers in your field, you'll have an inexhaustible "conversation" ongoing, so you'll not need to search for content to write about actively.

However, if you're still stuck, search for news articles related to your niche in the local newspaper or through sites like news.google.com and news.yahoo.com.

You can also have conversations with people who share your interests in the particular niche you choose, so you will eventually build up a bank of questions and answers and interesting discussions to write about in your blog. To do this, join forums related to your niche, but don't join every forum.

You can just stick with one or two with the most significant number of members or the one that is most focused on your niche. This will also come in handy much later in gaining traffic and generating profits.

Remember to keep up your momentum of posting at least once per day (or more if you have a lot of content to write about) so that the major search engines will know that your blog has fresh content every day.

This will attract the search engines to spider your page on a more frequent basis, hence gaining you extra traffic.

Don't worry about the paragraph above about generating traffic and search engines, because we're going to talk about that in more detail later. For now, remember to keep a consistent effort every day and build up momentum like that of a locomotive!

BLOGGING KNOWLEDGE

A blog is a website that 'publishes,' or features articles written by an individual or a group that make use of any or a combination of the following:

Straight texts

Photographs or images (photoblog)

Video (video blog)

Audio files (audio blog)

Hyperlinks

Usually presented and arranged in reverse chronological order, blogs are essentially used for the following purposes:

An online journal or a web diary.

Content management system.

Online publishing platform.

A typical blog has the following components:

Postdate -the date and time of the blog entry.

Category - the category that the blog belongs to.

Title - the title of the blog.

Main Body - the main content of the blog.

RSS and Trackback - links the blog back from other sites.

Comments - commentaries that are added by readers.

Permalinks - the URL of the full article.

Other Optional Items - calendar, archives, blogrolls, and addons or plug-ins.

A blog can also have a footer, usually found at the bottom of the blog, that shows the post date, the author, the category, and the 'stats' (the number of comments or trackbacks).

There are numerous types of blogs. Some of them are the following:

Political Blog - on news, politics, activism, and other issue-based blogs (such as campaigning).

Personal Blog - also known as online diary that may include an individual's day-to-day experience, complaints, poems, and illicit thoughts, and communications between friends.

Topical Blog - with focus either on a particular niche (function or position) that is usually technical in nature or a local information.

Literary Blog - also known as litblog.

Health Blog - on specific health issues. Medical blog is a major category of health blog that features medical news from health care professionals and/or actual patient cases.

Travel Blog - with focus on a traveler's stories on a particular journey.

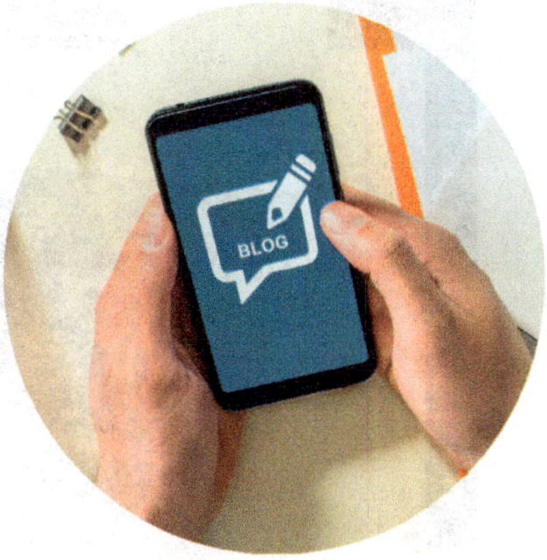

Travel Blog - with a focus on a traveler's stories on a particular journey.

Research Blog - on academic issues such as research notes.

Legal blog - on law (technical areas) and legal affairs; also known as 'blawgs.'

Media Blog- This type of blog focuses on falsehoods or inconsistencies in mass media, usually exclusive to newspapers or television networks.

Religious Blog - on religious topics.

Educational Blog - on educational applications, usually written by students and teachers.

Collaborative or Collective Blog - a specific topic written by a group.

Directory Blog - contains a collection of numerous websites.

Business Blog - used by entrepreneurs and corporate employees to promote businesses or discuss work.

Personification Blog - focus on non-human beings or objects (such as dogs).

Spam Blogs - used to promote affiliated websites; they are also known as 'splogs.'

Blogging is typically done on a regular (almost daily) basis. The term "blogging" refers to the act of authoring, maintaining, or adding an article to an existing blog, while the term "blogger" refers to a person or a group who keeps a blog.

Today, more than 3 million blogs can be found in the Internet. This figure is continuously growing, as the availability of various blog software, tools, and other applications make it easier for just about anyone to update or maintain the blog (even those with little or no technical background).

Because of this trend, bloggers can now be categorized into 4 main types:

Personal Bloggers - people who focus on a diary or on any topic that an individual feel strongly about.

Business Bloggers - people who focus on promoting products and services.

Organizational Bloggers - people who focus on internal or external communication in an organization or a community.

Professional Bloggers - people who are hired or paid to do blogging.

Problogging (professional blogging) refers to blogging for a profit. Probloggers (professional bloggers) are people who make money from blogging (as an individual blog publisher or a hired blogger).

Below are just some of the many money-making opportunities for probloggers:

Advertising programs

RSS advertising

Sponsorship

Affiliate Programs

Digital assets

Blog network writing gigs

Business blog writing gigs

Non blogging writing gigs

Donations

Flipping blogs

Merchandising

Consulting and speaking

The following are a few things that you need to consider if you want to be successful in pro blogging:

Be Patient - Problogging requires much time and effort, not to mention a long-term vision. The key to success in professional blogging is patience and a long-term vision. This requires a significant amount of time and effort

Know Your Audience - Targeting a specific audience or group is critical to building a readership.

Be An 'Expert' - Focus on a specific niche topic and strive to be the "go-to" blogger.

Please don't Bore Your Readers—focus on the layout. White spaces, line spacing, and bigger fonts make a blog welcoming to read.

Diversify—Experiment with various ads and affiliate programs that enable you to make money online (aside from blogging).

Indeed, it is possible to earn money from blogs. To be a successful blogger, one needs to take risks, be passionate, and have the right attitude.

Brain Dump

This is just a page for you to brain-dump any ideas, thoughts, questions, concerns or "research topics" that you plan to explore later.

Think Tank

6

Knowledge Sharing is Expensive

You produce quality over quantity, original content on your blog, and you will have attracted a decent amount of traffic.

To start generating profits from your blog's visitors, you must use Google's Adsense program correctly. Don't hesitate to visit their website and learn more about their advertising program. Here's a valuable tip:

Google's Adsense program is a highly effective way to make money from your blog. When readers finish reading your latest post, they may want to leave your blog. However, if your Adsense advertisement block is visible on your blog, they might see relevant ads and click on them, generating income for you.

Remember, if you don't use the program correctly, your profits will be minimal. Therefore, it's critical to place your Google ads in the right places and ensure they blend into your site to appear more like links than advertisements..

After obtaining a Google Adsense account, you have the option to modify the color of your advertisement text and links. It is advisable to match the colors of these ads with that of your blog's color scheme. For instance, if your blog's text is black and the links are red, ensure that the ad blocks' colors are also black and red respectively. This is a simple but effective way to make your ads blend in with your blog's design.

Another way to earn profits from your blog is to recommend products to your readers. When your visitors buy from the merchants you recommend, you also get to keep a little commission. This is known as affiliate marketing, and it is straightforward to start with because you don't have to create your own products or services. One way to earn money through your blog is by recommending products to your readers. By doing so, you can receive a commission when your visitors purchase products from the merchants you recommend. This is called affiliate marketing, and it's a simple way to get started because you don't have to create your own products or services.

Let's say you run a blog about technological gadgets, and you find a gadget called Gadget X on a merchant's website that offers an affiliate program. You can create a blog post and write a short review about Gadget X, highlighting its benefits and drawbacks, if any. You can also include a link provided by the merchant for visitors to purchase Gadget X online.

When your visitor clicks on the link and buys Gadget X, the merchant will track the purchase back to you, and you will receive a commission. If, for instance, you get 10,000 visitors each month, and 1 out of every 100 visitors purchases Gadget X, you could earn a commission of $27.00 from each purchase. This means you could earn a monthly income of $2,700.00 just by writing about one product.

To find affiliate programs related to your blog's theme, you can simply search on Google using the following query: "+affiliate program."

These are just some of the basic ways to generate income from your blog.

Additional Options for Profit

We've discussed about using Google Adsense program and other merchants' affiliate program to generate profits from your blog. However, we have a lot of other options to monetize your blog, so we're going to look into that now.

The first option we'll be looking at is Chitika (www.chitika.com). Chitika is a very innovative contextual advertising program because it can serve very detailed advertisements.

For example, on your technological gadget blog, Chitika will show advertisements for tech gadgets such as iPods. The way they show it is in different tabs: one for "Best deals", another for "details", another for "reviews" and so on.

This way, it is more of an informational section for your visitor rather than an advertisement, and naturally the click-through will be higher.

You can also be an affiliate for Amazon.com. Amazon offers a wide range of products, but its predominant domain is in books. Whatever your niche is about, you can probably find a book about it on Amazon.com.

Once you join them, you can refer visitors to them and earn up to 7% commission. It's not a lot, but if you can manage to refer significant volumes of visitors, Amazon is for you. This program really shines when it comes to the ways you can refer visitors: you can use their predefined templates to pull up recent items that match specific criteria you set, you can target your ad to show a specific item on sale, or you can just simply weave your referral links into your blog posts.

Last but definitely not least, you can sell advertising space on your blog if it is truly popular. If you manage to pull in huge amounts of traffic like that blog, you can definitely get people to buy ad space on your blog for prices from $150/month upwards, depending on its popularity.

To gauge how many pageviews and visitors you get daily, just use the free tool available at statcounter.com. They have a detailed setup guide there, so I won't investigate it.

If your blog has not acquired a large number of visitors yet, you can still sell ad space on it on a per-click or per-impression basis. Just visit sites like adbrite.com.

Hopefully, that will help you maximize earnings and profits from your blog!

Brain Dump

This is just a page for you to brain-dump any ideas, thoughts, questions, concerns or "research topics" that you plan to explore later.

Think Tank

7

Game Changing

"Videoblogging is the new way of sharing ideas and promoting products on the internet."

Everybody knows about textblogging. Now they use videos for a better way of expression. This form of communication may entail a lot of resources, but it is all worth it. If pictures say a thousand words, videoblogging exceeds that by far.

A videoblog requires larger disk spaces on websites, a faster server, and a whole new set of programs to support it. Videoblogs can be fed through RSS. This is technology of syndicating your website to other RSS aggregators.

Videoblogging works with people on the internet expressing their selves. Now if you put this on a business prospective, you are up to a lot of benefits. Think of it as a powerful tool in making showing your prospective customers your line of products or your services. It's just like showing a commercial all for free. And if you videoblog through RSS, then most probably you are getting your target market.

People like to see what they are going to buy. Some would like to see proof and be sure that they are getting their money's worth before shelving their dimes on it.

All of us know the influence of a thirty second commercial. The effect of videoblogging is similar to that. You show your product, people watch it. If they like it, they buy it. If you present it good enough, they'll buy the product even if they don't need it.

Now, on the web, things are static, unlike on television, which all move. If you post something mobile, it will most likely catch your attention. Now, imagine your product parading in all its royalty through videoblog. You'll get phone call orders in no time.

If you're starting a business and want to create a videoblog, you can easily do it from the comfort of your own home. All you need is a web camera, microphone, video editing software, and some lights. As long as you know how to use your camera, you can create a great video blog.

It's important to invest in a good web camera with a high resolution for the best output. This will help in presenting your goods in the best possible way. You can create a short story or capture your goods in one go, but make sure you're getting the best profile for each. Let your creativity flow!

Lights are also important in production. Ensure that the area you're recording in is well-lit for crisp and clear images. You can also use lighting effects to add appeal to your presentation.

If you need to add sound to your videoblog, you'll need a microphone. Record your voice as a voiceover to promote the product and its benefits to consumers. Sounds are just as important as videos on a videoblog, so it's best to make your sound effects as enticing as the video itself.

Any video editing software will do for finalizing your work. You can add sounds, delete bad angles, or insert still pictures. Some programs are user-friendly and can be used even with zero knowledge of video editing.

Video editing programs are crucial for creating impressive videos. It's highly essential to choose the right background that complements the lighting and enhances the presentation.

Videoblogging is a powerful tool that can be used to promote your brand. Although it may slow down your computer and take longer to download, it's worth the effort. Don't let these challenges hinder you from using videoblogging as part of your marketing strategy. However, ensure that you include text and pictures to cater to your diverse audience.

In today's world, creativity plays a vital role in marketing success. Videoblogging offers an interactive way to showcase your products and their advantages. It enables you to engage with your customers and make them part of the selling process. With this approach, you can make sales and succeed in your business.

The way a blog is written can make all the difference between a profitable and non-profitable one. Consider this - would you rather read a university professor's lecture notes or the latest novel by your favorite author? Most people would choose the novel because it is more interesting and less boring than lecture notes.

When people visit your blog, they are not only looking for information but also for information that is easy to digest and presented in a relaxed manner. To attract more visitors and keep current ones coming back, it is important to add a human touch to your blog posts.

You can achieve this by imagining that you are having a conversation about a certain topic with a personal friend. Additionally, humor can be a great way to engage your readers, so try to include funny comments in your articles where appropriate.

It's also important to address your readers in a singular rather than plural form. Rather than writing as if you were delivering a speech, aim to create a personal connection with your readers.

When writing for your blog, it is important to address your readers as if you are having a conversation with a single person. This approach can help create a more personalized and friendly tone, which can make it easier for your readers to connect with you and your content.

Moreover, it is crucial to establish your own unique personality through your writing. Readers are naturally curious and will be interested in learning more about you, in addition to the information you provide. Developing a distinctive voice for your blog can set it apart from other similar blogs on the same topic.

Think of it as creating your own brand. If readers associate your blog with a reputable source of information on a particular topic, you have successfully created a brand. Similar to how people associate McDonald's with fast food or Nike with sportswear.

To sum up, when writing for your blog, aim to create a friendly and personal tone while also establishing your own unique voice to differentiate your blog from others.

Monthly *Blog Planner*

Date :

Month :

MONTHS PRIORITY

TO DO LIST

MON	TUE	WED	THU	FRI	SAT	SUN

Clearing House

This is just a page for you to fill the house with ideas, thoughts, questions, concerns or research topics that you plan to explore at a later date.

What's Next?

Book Launch

www.fdyconsultants.com

Made in the USA
Monee, IL
02 November 2026

67380385R00044